ITALY IN LOVE ♥

ART AND BEAUTY PRESS

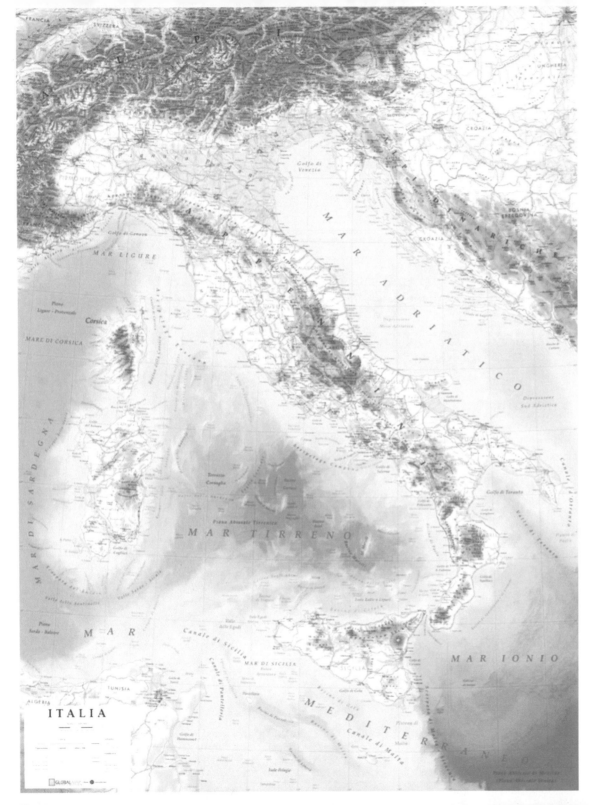

Italy is an incredible land that take your breath away.

Nestled in the Mediterranean Sea, offers beautiful landscapes between sea and mountains, and between lakes and forests.

Here you can find the best beaches and the best food in the world.

Be overwhelmed by the beauty of this country; you will fall in love immediately.

Are you ready for this amazing travel?

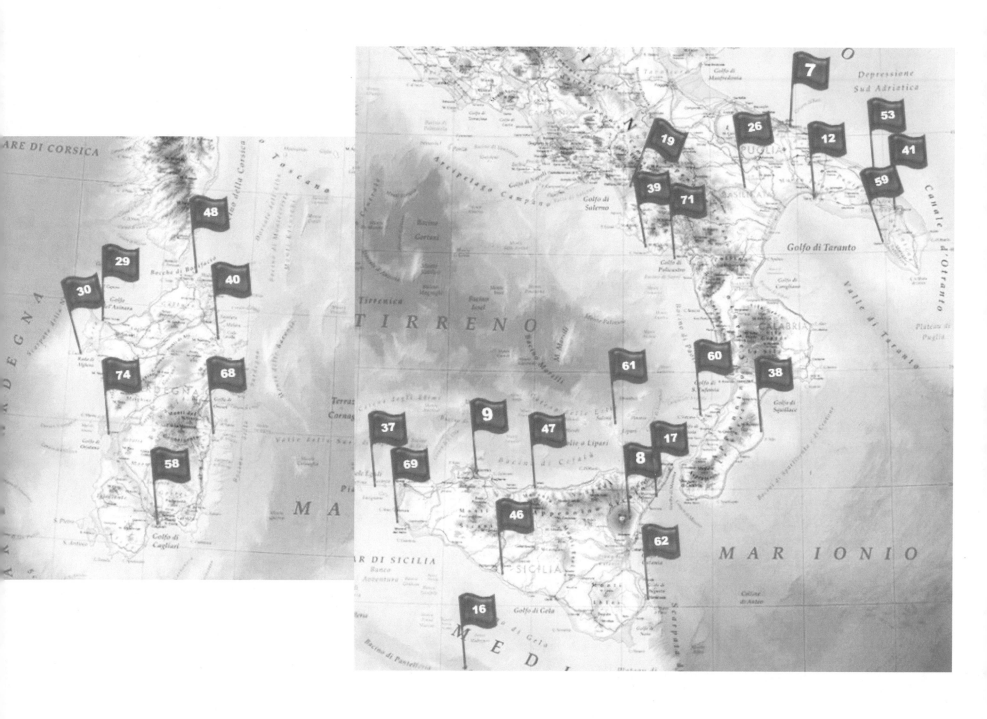

1-Venez

2-Roma

3-Napo

4-Firenze

5-Milan

6-Torino

7-Bari

8-Catania

9-Palerm

10-Bologna

11-Genov

12-Taranto

13-Cinque Terre

14-Parma

15-Sien

16-Lampedusa

17-Taormina

18-Pompei

19-Paestum

20-Viterbo

21-Assi

22-Perugia

23-Ercolan

24-Vasto

25-Ostia Antic

26-Matera

27-Isola d'Ischia

28-Isola di Procida

29-Stintino

30-Alghero

31-Capri

32-Padova

33-Marostica

34-Isola d'Elba

35-Aosta

36-Bolzano

37-Favignana

38-Soverato

39-Palinuro

40-Costa Smeralda

41-Lecce

42-Amalfi

43-Positano

44-Sorrento

45-Rimini

46-Agrigento

47-Cefalù

48-Arcipelago della Maddalena

49-Trani

50-Pisa

51-Lucca

52-Trieste

53-Brindisi

54-Ravenna

55-Ferrara

56-Sanremo

57-Argentari

58-Cagliari

59-Gallipoli

60-Tropea

61-Stromboli

62-Siracusa

63-Vieste

64-Polignano

65-Lago Trasimeno

66-Bellagio

67-Ponza

68-Arbatax

69-Marsala

70-Bergamo

71-Maratea

72-Ancona

73-Sulmona

74-Bosa

ITALY IN LOVE 🖤

CPSIA information can be obtained
at www.ICGtesting.com
Printed in the USA
BVRC100958260421
605862BV00011B/261